Not Afraid

Jill P. Boyce

Not Afraid
Copyright © 2005
Jill P. Boyce
Dream Creations, Inc.
www.dreamci.com
1-866-823-8501

Library of Congress — In Cataloging

Printed in the United States

Clark's Graphics & Publications
Clarkspublications@comcast.net
972-424-2074 (office)

Cover: U.S. Army Photo by Spc. Brian Schroeder

Dedication

I dedicate this book to my mother, Joan Davis Precht
(1930-1998), who taught me that true happiness
comes only when we are helping others.

"To ease another's heartache is to forget one's own."

Abraham Lincoln

Acknowledgements

Thank you to Chaplain Jim Combs and his wife Lisa and their children – my prayer assignment and many times, my inspiration to keep going. My daughters, Amber, Chrissy, and Melissa and their families have been helpful and supportive, loving me through this busy time. Shirley Clark, an angel sent from God to help me get this book published right on time, has been a great inspiration to me. Norma Anderson, who led me gently through a tough assignment in a very short time, not only editing but mentoring as well in the process, has made this book possible. I especially thank our military men and women and their families – the "forgotten soldiers" – for their great sacrifice for the freedom our country enjoys.

Table of Contents

Psalm 91 – The Words
Introduction

These powerful words changed my life. I pray they will change yours, too.

PSALM 91

He who dwells in the secret place of the Most High
Shall abide under the shadow of the Almighty.
I will say of the Lord, He is my refuge and my fortress;
My God, in Him I will trust.
Surely He shall deliver me from the snare of the fowler
And from the perilous pestilence.
He shall cover me with His feathers,
And under His wings I shall take refuge;
His truth shall be my shield and buckler.
I shall not be afraid of the terror by night,
Nor of the arrow that flies by day,
Nor of the pestilence that walks in darkness,
Nor of the destruction that lays waste at noonday.
A thousand may fall at my side,
And ten thousand at my right hand;
But it shall not come near me.
Only with my eyes shall I look and see the
reward of the wicked.
Because I have made the Lord, Who is my refuge,
Even the Most High, my dwelling place,
No evil shall befall me, Nor shall any plague
come near my dwelling;
For He shall give His angels charge over me,
To keep me in all my ways.
In their hands they shall bear me up,
Lest I dash my foot against a stone.
I shall tread upon the lion and the cobra,
The young lion and the serpent I shall
trample underfoot.
Because I have set my love upon Him,
therefore He will deliver me;
He will set me on high because I have known His name.
I shall call upon Him, and He will answer me.
He will be with me in trouble; He will deliver me
and honor me.
With long life He will satisfy me and show
me His salvation.

Jill P. Boyce © 2003

Introduction

In Honor of Our Military

Photo provided by Chaplain (MAJ) J. Craig Combs

This book is written in honor of the men and women defending our freedom, in all arms of the military—whether overseas on the battlefield, at a desk on base, attending the wounded in a hospital, or at a training or recruiting facility. We are proud of you. We need you. We are behind you. If it weren't for you and your comrades who have served before you, our country would not be free, and the world would be filled with dictators of every sort, ruling the people with iron fists.

"The hardest battle that ever was fought
Shall I tell you where or when?
On the maps of the world you will find it not
'Twas fought by the mothers of men."

Author Unknown

Description of a Soldier

Excerpts from an email sent by a soldier's mother:

The average age of the military man is 19 years. He is 10 or 15 pounds lighter now than when he was at home because he is working or fighting from before dawn to well after dusk.

He has trouble spelling, thus letter writing is a pain for him, but he can field strip a rifle in 30 seconds and reassemble it in less time in the dark. He digs foxholes and latrines and can apply first aid like a professional. He can march until he is told to stop or stop until he is told to march.

He obeys orders instantly and without hesitation, but he is not without spirit or individual dignity. He is self-sufficient. He has two sets of fatigues: he washes one and wears the other. He keeps his canteens full and his feet dry. He sometimes forgets to brush his teeth, but never to clean his rifle. He can cook his own meals, mend his own clothes, and fix his own hurts. If you're thirsty, he'll share his water with you; if you are hungry, his food. He'll even split his ammunition with you in the midst of battle when you run low.

He has wept in public and in private, for friends who have fallen in combat and is unashamed. He feels every note of the National Anthem vibrate through his body while at rigid attention, while tempering the burning desire to "square-away" those around him who haven't bothered to stand, remove their hat, or even stop talking. In an odd twist, day in and day out, far from home, he defends their right to be disrespectful. Just as did his father, grandfather, and great-grandfather, he is paying the price for our freedom. Beardless or not, he is not a boy. He is the American Fighting Man that has kept this country free for over 200 years. He has asked nothing in return, except our friendship and understanding. Remember him always, for he has earned our respect and admiration with his blood. And now we even have women over there in danger, doing their part in this tradition of going to war when our nation calls us to do so.

Of all the gifts you could give a U.S. Soldier, Sailor, Coastguardsman, Marine or Airman, <u>prayer</u> is the very best one.

"Lord, hold our troops in your loving hands. Protect them as they protect us. Bless them and their families for the selfless acts they perform for us in our time of need. Amen."

Chapter 1

The Dream

THERE I WAS STANDING IN IRAQ, SIX WEEKS BE-
FORE THE WAR BEGAN, JUST THIS SIDE OF
THE IRAQI/KUWAITI BORDER. Surrounded by our soldiers who were fighting Saddam Hussein's Iraqi army, I
heard the sounds of war all around me. It was as though I
could reach out and touch the people, but I was invisible
to them. What I witnessed in the dream was awful. I saw
injured and dying men all around me.

Waking at 3:30 a.m., I was shaking but not really
afraid. I felt that this was a warning of what could happen
if people did not pray. Immediately, I knew I had to pray
that this scenario would not take place when our men and
women went to fight for freedom in Iraq. I had a sense
that others around the world were praying the same
prayer. I continued praying until I fell asleep. The dream
was so authentic. I will never forget it. The memory of it is
etched in my mind. I felt I had to do something.

The next day, I had an idea. I envisioned a camouflage bandana with the words from Psalm 91 printed
down the middle. I went to my Bible to look it up. As a for-
mer first grade teacher, I had worked with my students in

memorizing the first part of this Psalm. Now I was curious to know what it had to do with our military. As I read the words, I realized it had been written for soldiers and others in dangerous situations.

You shall not be afraid of the terror by night,
Nor of the arrow that flies by day...

Psalms 91:5

I had heard stories about groups of soldiers from previous wars reading or memorizing Psalm 91. These stories gave me courage to pursue the dream. I began to surf the web to get more information. It was abounding with stories of how God had protected soldiers from death and injury throughout World War I and World War II, along with Vietnam, Korea and the previous Gulf War, Desert Storm. Many of these soldiers had embraced Psalm 91 and returned home from the war alive and well. My faith began to grow as I realized God wanted me to get bandanas imprinted with Psalm 91 and get them to as many soldiers as I could. My strategy was to get them out to the troops before the Iraqi war began.

I found military bandanas and purchased a few at a local craft store. Using an embroidery hoop for tautness, I wrote the scripture on these bandanas with a permanent marker. I gave these prototypes to the prayer pastor at my local church and to other key people. I valued their insight and wise counsel.

Two or three prayer groups that I attended purposefully prayed with me about this new project. Several friends gave donations to buy more bandanas. I could feel God's power working for me and through me. All this time, I felt that war was imminent. It was urgent to get the bandanas to the troops as quickly as possible.

I emailed the President of the United States with my idea and a copy of Psalm 91, stating that in my opinion some of the words were in direct reference to germ and chemical warfare.

**You shall not be afraid...of the pestilence
that walks in darkness or of the destruction that
lays waste at noonday.
No evil shall befall you, nor shall any
plague come near your dwelling.**

Psalms 91:5,6,10

I received an "auto-responder" message from the President's office thanking me for my email.

After many frustrations, I finally found a way to print the bandanas. A friend suggested having them screen-printed. I bought a few bandanas at local Army/Navy stores around Dallas and had them printed up at a local shop.

Right about that time, an Army recruiter called my home in hopes of signing up my daughter Melissa, a recent high school graduate. I told him about my dream and the bandanas, and my determination to get them to the troops before war broke out. The recruiter suggested I call Fort Hood. This Army base is just a few hours south of my home in the Dallas area. I called the Fort Hood directory and asked for the chaplain's office.

In my naivety, I had no idea that Fort Hood is the size of a city. It is the largest military installation in the free world. There are several chaplains' offices. Somehow, I was given the phone number of Chaplain Jim Combs. After talking to him, I emailed him my idea. He emailed me back saying that he liked the idea

My faith began to grow as I realized God wanted me to get bandanas imprinted with Psalm 91 and get them to as many soldiers as I could.

and was passing it on to his superiors. Amazingly, I was able to send my first shipment of 79 bandanas to Fort Hood. Meanwhile, the war had started in Iraq.

During that time, I just happened to get the largest income tax refund I had ever received. I ordered 840 bandanas from Carolina Manufacturing. Printing them locally allowed me to pick them up within 24 hours. The news media kept announcing that men and women from Fort Hood would be deployed in the next few days. I decided to take the day off work and deliver the bandanas to Fort Hood myself.

Chaplain Combs invited me to come on base and give them out individually. Some troops were leaving the following day. Imagine my surprise when I received a plaque for service to the Army from Chaplain Combs that day. I was completely humbled. My daughter Chrissy accompanied me on the trip and took some pictures of Chaplain Combs, Chaplain Stroop and Chaplain Assistants, Sergeant Kelly and Sergeant Diaz.

Chaplains at Fort Hood
March 2003

After that overwhelming experience, I continued to personally deliver the bandanas to Fort Hood. The troops, including both men and women, were deploying too quickly for me to ship the bandanas. The largest delivery was 1,500 bandanas.

Soon, President Bush gave his famous speech from the <u>USS</u> <u>Abraham Lincoln</u>, declaring "major combat operations in Iraq have ended." I immediately saw a change in the attitude of people around me in North Texas. It was as though they almost forgot about our troops. Many loved ones on the frontlines defending our freedom were being forgotten. In the midst of this, I continued to receive emails from chaplains and others requesting bandanas for the soldiers. Deployments to Iraq and Afghanistan were happening regularly.

About the time President Bush made his speech, I was invited to a "Division Prayer Breakfast" at the Fort Hood Officers' Club. I was the only civilian present. A Psalm 91 bandana was at each place setting as a gift for the attendees. This was an unexpected honor. I was happy to find out Chaplain Combs would be attending with me, but after we arrived, he slipped away to another table and left me with some very impressive officers at one of the front tables. I felt that I was in the presence of greatness.

I was grateful for the plaque, prayer breakfast and all the "thank yous"... but I still had a mission... *to get a Psalm 91 bandana into the hands of every military person who wanted one.*

Chapter 2

No Way To Help

During these last years of witnessing our men and women deploying to Iraq and Afghanistan, one thing I have noticed is how much the chaplains care about those in their charge. It is not just a job to them. It is a way of life–making sure their men and women are well taken care of, comforted and counseled.

My first example of that deep level of commitment was Chaplain (MAJ) Phillip Glick, a National Guardsman and Episcopal priest from Richmond, Virginia. After the major offensive of March and April of 2003, our men and women were still being sent overseas, and they still needed prayer and support. I became aware of this need as I continued to get requests for Psalm 91 bandanas from chaplains.

I remember receiving a request from Chaplain Glick – bandanas for approximately 400 soldiers in his charge. Not a single penny was left for purchasing more bandanas. The contributions seemed to just dry up. I had done everything I knew to do to raise money for more bandanas, but to no avail. I sat at my computer and cried, asking God to provide. I did not know how I could respond to Chaplain Glick knowing that he would be disappointed.

I decided to reply to Chaplain Glick with the truth. I had no bandanas left and no money to buy more. I would be praying, I told him. A while later, he replied, "I'm going home on leave, and I will try to raise the money for the bandanas we need."

A short time later, Chaplain Glick notified me that his church and several others in the area had come up with the necessary funds to pay for the bandanas. It was the first time I had ever sold any bandanas. I felt guilty, but relieved. After all, I felt that my ministry was to *give* *away* the bandanas – not *sell* them.

I prayed that somehow God would help me get bandanas to them.

Right before he deployed to Iraq, Chaplain Glick met me in Dallas where he was visiting friends and picked up the bandanas. His determination and loyalty to his men and women were inspiring.

Later that summer, another chaplain who had seen the bandanas at the prayer breakfast at Fort Hood emailed to order some. He was now stationed at Fort Drum in New York. Again, I was unable to help because of the large amount needed. When this chaplain and his soldiers deployed to Afghanistan, I prayed that somehow God would help me get Psalm 91 bandanas to them soon.

As it turned out, with sales of the bandanas in the fall, I was able to save up enough to purchase the almost 400 bandanas to send over in Christmas packages. My daughters helped me pack candy canes, Christmas cards and bandanas into boxes. After tracking down Father Bob Pleczkowski, we mailed him the Christmas packages as a surprise. Not long afterwards, I received an email expressing gratitude with photos of them and their gifts. God had answered my prayer, but in His own time and His own way.

Several of my friends and prayer partners counseled me to find a way to offer the bandanas for sale at post exchanges throughout the world so that men and women could more easily get them before deploying. My friend Alicia introduced me to Chaplain (COL) Jim Ammerman, U.S. Army (Retired). He let me know he would be glad to help with this challenging project.

With his help, I was able to make an appointment with an officer at the Army Air Force Exchange Services (AAFES), headquartered in Dallas, Texas. Chaplain Ammerman was kind enough to accompany me when I met with AAFES buyers to present the bandanas. Fumbling through my presentation, I soon realized I was in way over my head. Competing with large companies and offering only one small product, I am sure it seemed like a ridiculous item to offer for sale in military exchanges. By the looks on their faces I could tell there was just no way to get my product into the military exchanges. After all, I was an elementary teacher, not a sales person.

At that point, I do not remember what was said, but I believe that God intervened somehow. Suddenly, the tone changed. A list of possible ways to make my product available was offered. I could fill out paperwork and get permission to sell the bandanas in the mall outside the Fort Hood main PX, offer my product for sale at their online site or sign up with a military distributor. They gave me two companies to contact. I thanked them for their time. I told Chaplain Ammerman how much I appreciated his help.

I have met my share of people, and I can honestly say that I have never met anyone with as big a dose of the character and love of Christ as this man. I am eternally grateful for his strategic role in getting the Psalm 91 bandana out to the troops.

Soon I was able to begin selling the bandanas at Fort Hood right outside the main PX inside the mall area. During the several weeks when I was there, I had the honor of meeting soldiers, airmen and veterans, along with their families, wives and children. People were wonderful, and I could see how much they were open to God. I started a prayer list and asked soldiers for their first names so I could pray for them. They seemed happy to be added to my list.

The bandanas sold like hotcakes! I could not keep enough in supply! Not only did soldiers purchase them, but also wives, mothers, fathers, and children. I remember a young man about 12 years old who scraped together enough money to buy one for his mother to have while his dad was overseas. (She had already bought one to send to her husband.)

No matter what kind of religious beliefs the people had, they all liked the Psalm 91 bandana. After a couple of months of great sales figures, Brigade Quartermasters, one of the companies I had contacted, agreed to begin selling the product. This was the way to get them into PX's all over the world!

By November of 2003, Brigade Quartermasters, a wholesale military supply company, was distributing the bandanas, making them available to the military on a large scale. I personally believe that God used this company and its President, Mitchell L. WerBell, in a strategic way to distribute the Psalm 91 bandanas to families and friends of military men and women everywhere. I will always be grateful to Mitchell and his fine staff as they helped me with my mission to make the bandanas available to anyone who wanted them. I have personally talked to several soldiers and civilians who have seen the bandanas in PX's in Iraq and have been thankful for their availability.

"The 91st Psalm Bandana created by Jill Boyce has become more than a novelty; it is a morale necessity for the Armed Forces going into harm's way around the world. Jill's determination is a force on its own and through her persistence, we were able to help make her dream a reality. More than 150,000 bandanas have been sold through the Army & Air Force and Marine Corps Exchange stores worldwide. Thousands more have been donated by many organizations to the troops headed into combat. One of the most important things all Americans can do is to let the troops know we care and pray for them. Having the 91st Psalm, close to heart provides immeasurable spiritual comfort, and we are glad to have been a part of getting the mission accomplished."

Mitchell L. WerBell, IV
President, Brigade Quartermasters, Ltd

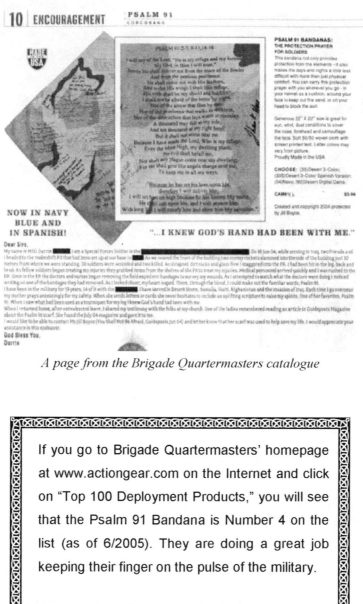

A page from the Brigade Quartermasters catalogue

If you go to Brigade Quartermasters' homepage at www.actiongear.com on the Internet and click on "Top 100 Deployment Products," you will see that the Psalm 91 Bandana is Number 4 on the list (as of 6/2005). They are doing a great job keeping their finger on the pulse of the military.

Chapter 3

The Adventure Begins

In December 2003, I found out that Chaplain (CPT) James "Jim" Combs of the 1st Cavalry Division would be deploying soon to Iraq, along with thousands of other men and women from Fort Hood. I had previously emailed him about the bandana. They anticipated being gone a little over a year. I was waiting on a tentative chaplaincy order from Fort Hood that would provide Psalm 91 bandanas for deploying troops who wanted them. There had been a hold-up, so I began scrambling to raise money for Chaplain Combs' group of approximately 500. The original order had difficulties going through for some strange reason, but we were able to get the bandanas needed for Chaplain Combs' men. He wanted to offer them to the men at the time of departure, so I left them with him to distribute.

Meanwhile, Karen, the wife of another soldier, Sergeant Chuck Hreha, called to see if there was any way I could provide bandanas for his group of approximately 300. God provided a way to do that through December sales of the bandana. Delivery came in plenty of time for the color-casing ceremony on the parade grounds of the base. Karen invited me to attend with her and then help give out the bandanas to the men following the ceremony. The experience was unforgettable as I watched the men and women of several brigades marching past as I sat in the stands surrounded by their family members and friends. In a color-casing ceremony, the flags (colors) of the deploying units are placed in canvas "cases" symbolizing the end of the units' current mission. The colors are "uncased" when the units arrive at their new location to begin their new mission. The act of casing the colors is symbolic of the units' journey.

After the first of the year, Chuck's group and Chaplain Combs' group deployed to Iraq. After having prayed with the Combs family, I promised Jim I would help Lisa as much as possible while he was gone.

Lisa and I emailed each other from time to time and sometimes talked on the phone. During one of these talks, she suggested that I write and submit a story to Guideposts magazine about how God gave me the dream and idea for the Psalm 91 bandana. I had read Guideposts for years, and I really did not think they would be interested in my story. Lisa said she originally thought of writing it, but with five children and all the duties of two parents now, she would not have time. I told her I would consider it. That night, I sat down at the computer and wrote out the whole story the best that I could remember. I emailed it to Lisa for her opinion. She liked it. After looking up <u>Guideposts</u>' submission guidelines online, I made some changes and sent it off along with a Psalm 91 bandana.

Their response was quick. They loved it and wanted to publish it in the July 2004 issue. It was like a dream come true because I grew up reading the stories in <u>Guideposts</u> magazine. I always secretly wanted to write a story myself someday.

Things were quiet for a while concerning the bandanas. What I did not know was that the adventure had really just begun.

Chapter 4

The Forgotten Soldiers

As things continued to develop with the bandanas, I came to know some of the family members, and it seemed that they really needed encouragement. A customer, Mary Martinez, called me one evening to place a bulk order at a discount price. She and her Family Readiness Group wanted to sell the bandanas at retail and use the money to get away from the base for a weekend with their families just to be refreshed and gain some peace. I mentioned to her that I had been trying to find a way to help military families and that I had just finished a phone conversation with a friend who suggested getaway weekends for military spouses and children.

Mary's husband, Staff Sergeant Michael Martinez, was in Iraq at the time, having deployed a little ahead of Chaplain Combs' group and Chuck Hreha's group. Mary and I brainstormed for almost two hours on the phone as I kept notes on our conversation. Within ten days of that brainstorming session, we had formed a nonprofit corporation, Deployed Soldiers Family Foundation (DSFF), and begun the task of planning our first retreat for families. We like to call these military families the "Forgotten Soldiers."

It wasn't easy, since we were new at all this, but we had some great people surrounding us and helping us, with Lisa Combs and Mary working on things at Fort Hood and some friends of mine helping me in Dallas.

On Armed Forces Day, May 21, 2004, just two months after the inception of the organization, we held our first getaway for military spouses and children from Fort Hood. The families were from Mike Martinez's military intelligence unit.

It wasn't easy, since we were new at all this, but we had some great people surrounding us and helping us.

They arrived on Friday evening after work and school, registered and enjoyed a light meal. The next day, some of the teens went to Six Flags with parents while the ladies were treated to new hairstyles, manicures, chair massages, and makeup sessions for a complete makeover. Mannatech, a company based in the Dallas area, helped sponsor the event at the Sheraton Grand DFW. They even sent volunteers including a photographer and videographer!

One of the fun things the kids got to do was go to the Build-A-Bear store at Grapevine Mills Mall and "build" their own bears. The folks there at Build-A-Bear were eager to help encourage military families, so they donated the bears to make all this possible. The children had a great time and got the chance to pick out their own outfits and accessories for the stuffed bears. One little girl dressed her bear up in Army fatigues and named him after her daddy so she could feel like he was right there with her. She said that her daddy had always carried her on his shoulders, but now she could carry him on hers.

On Saturday evening, we had a dinner to honor the spouses, and even though we provided a separate dinner for the kids, some of the teens showed up to escort their mothers. We enjoyed entertainment. Then Captain Al Crawford spoke to us about the military R & R program that was just beginning at the Dallas/Fort Worth airport. He explained a little about how the men and women coming home on leave would arrive and depart from there. He told us about the new USO facility that was being built and established there to give the men and women a place to go while waiting for their flights. The DFW Airport is one of the facilities in the United States that receives our deployed troops coming home for their two week breaks.

The weekend ended with the families being on their own to shop, sightsee or return home. All in all, I would say the weekend was a success. Our goal for these weekends is to ease the tension and show the families that we care about them and their loved ones overseas defending our freedom. I believe that was accomplished.

In August, our second getaway weekend took place at the Omni Park West on the edge of Dallas. Over 300 deployed soldiers' wives and children enjoyed a spa weekend free of charge. This time, my friend Patty Logan organized a style show for the spouses to enjoy while eating lunch. It was a highlight of their weekend. The school-age children were entertained with exclusive use of a local game and recreation facility with food, games, and a movie. That night, at the hotel, they chowed down on hot dogs during movie time while their moms had the opportunity to go out to eat at local area restaurants. We even had an awesome group of volunteer nursery workers that weekend providing tender loving care for the little ones. Here are some of the testimonials we received from those who attended the DSFF weekends and even a letter from a parent.

Thank you for a wonderful weekend getaway!

Ehorri M.

I've been both deployed soldier and the spouse back home, and from my viewpoint, it's a lot tougher on the spouse.

Krista B.

Since January, it seems, I have forgotten how to smile and laugh. Over the last few days, I talked, I listened, I laughed (and then laughed some more)....I leave with the smile back in my heart, and that is the most wonderful gift of all. Thank you.

Kathy D.

My first-born son is serving in Iraq as an Infantry Company Commander in the First Cavalry Division. Your organization did a marvelous thing in providing a Dallas weekend for my daughter-in-law. She expressed tremendous appreciation for the support y'all gave so generously. Thanks for all you are doing!

Paul B.

Thank you for providing families the opportunity to "get away from it all." I have talked with my husband, and the weekend away positively affected the morale of the troops...just knowing that their families are happy and having a great time does wonders.

S.J.

I would like this opportunity to again thank all who were involved either by being there, organizing things, or donating items. This has been a weekend I will never forget. You have thought not only of the spouses, but the children, and our soldiers overseas. I can truly relay that my husband was impressed and very grateful for this event. The kindness of all who were involved in making this weekend so special was unforgettable. I can honestly say I have never been around such caring people.

R. F.

We cannot control what's going on in Iraq or Afghanistan or anywhere else in the world that our soldiers may be deployed to in the future, but we <u>can</u> do something to encourage them. One way I have found is to help their families, the "Forgotten Soldiers," handle the added stress by treating them to these wellness weekends away from the base. This can be done in cities all over the United States.

If you would like more information about Deployed Soldiers Family Foundation, you can go to our website, www.dsffusa.org or call us at 1-866-823-8501.

Chapter 5

Bandanas Everywhere!

N ot long after we established Deployed Soldiers Family Foundation (DSFF) and held our first retreat for soldiers' families, the Guideposts article I had submitted back in January came out in the July issue. My dad called me the evening of June 26 to prepare me for a possible flood of phone calls for orders. He mentioned that he had received his July Guideposts already and that the circulation for the magazine was several million. I braced myself and had my shipping materials ready, but I was not prepared for the deluge of phone calls, emails and online orders I received during the months of July and August.

In those last four days of June alone, I processed over 200 orders. I quickly realized I would need more help. I had just hired an assistant who had earlier volunteered to help me with DSFF. I had signed up with an online bookstore that a friend of mine had introduced me to. If God had not brought my administrative assistant, Sri Prabhakar, and Spread the Word Ministries into my life at precisely the right moment, I could not have kept up with the orders. Sri helped me fill out orders and package them as well as set up a database for my new customers. The Spread the Word folks did a great job keeping up with all the online orders.

The phone never stopped ringing. I would hang up, and it would ring immediately. At the end of each day, I checked messages, which consisted of order after order. I took calls from early in the morning from customers on the East Coast to late in the evening from West Coast customers. Sometimes, when there was a lull in calls, I was able to visit with the people. I talked

Before October was over, the bandana craziness had started again! We had orders coming in faster than I could handle them.

to wives, mothers, fathers, sisters, brothers, and grandparents of military men and women. I can still remember many of their names. They were always happy to give me their loved ones' names to add to my prayer wall. Sometimes, we said a prayer together. They were the most wonderful people!

Church groups called to place orders. They wanted the bandanas to add to packages they were sending to their members in Iraq or Afghanistan. Chaplains called to order for their units. Civic groups and organizations wanted bandanas to send to the troops overseas or to give to those deploying. It was phenomenal!

Even with help during the day, I could not get my orders out in time. I would work until late at night and through the weekends. One weekend, I had the whole family over for pizza and fulfillment of bandana orders. They helped me write orders, cut poem cards and count bandanas as they slipped them into packages. After pizza, a movie, and a few hours of work, we had it all done. Once they helped me catch up and we got our system down, things went so much more smoothly. I'll always be thankful for their help.

I remember when I received my first order inquiry from Baghdad. It was from Army Chaplain Reese Hutcheson of the 89th Military Police Brigade. He said he had a bandana with Psalm 91 printed on it and that his brigade commander was interested in buying one for every soldier in the brigade. I gave him the information he needed to make a military purchase through my wholesaler, Brigade Quartermasters.

As the months went on, the bandana orders kept coming in. During that summer, Guideposts magazine called me to see how things were going. It indicated to me that they had received numerous inquiries and phone calls as a result of the July article. I told them how busy I had been and the story about my children and others coming to help me. They said they

wanted to do a follow-up article in the November magazine. By that time, I was in the middle of working on our
second DSFF getaway for soldiers' families that would
take place at the end of August.

The next couple of months were fairly quiet al-
though the orders continued to stream in. Before October was over, the bandana craziness had started again!
From the last week in October through the middle of December, we had orders coming in faster than I could
handle them. Again, God intervened and sent a wonderful friend, Nora Torres, to help me with my orders. It was
busy, but a time of real blessing. What I enjoyed most
about taking orders was the chance to talk to family
members and friends of our military men and women.

Chapter 6

I Shall Not Be Afraid

Master Sergeant Darrin Crowder

Photo provided by Darrin Crowder

Master Sergeant Darrin Crowder is a 20-year veteran of the United States Army. For over 15 years he served as a Green Beret with the 5th Special Forces Group (Airborne) throughout the Middle East and Africa. He has seen combat during the Gulf War, Somalia, Haiti, Afghanistan, and two tours in Iraq. His service awards and decorations number over 60 including three Bronze Stars for valor of service, the Purple Heart, the Combat Infantry Badge, Static Line and Military Freefall Jump Master Badges, and numerous other United States and Foreign decorations.

I had a bad feeling about heading overseas, even though I had been involved in plenty of dangerous situations in countries all over the world. The weekend before my deployment to Iraq, my family helped me pack up my belongings. Before my mom hugged me goodbye, she asked if I felt okay about going. I faked a smile and said I would be just fine. When she went out to the car to leave, I handed my sister Denyne all of my important papers and confided in her that I did not feel good about this trip. I knew she would not tell Mom as it would just worry her.

Over the 18 years I had served in the Army, Mom had always written to me. Each letter ended with,

"Be good, be careful, and live for the Lord. I'm praying for you. I love you. ~ Momma."

Then down at the bottom there would always be a scripture verse to encourage me, like Psalm 91.

On Wednesday, June 10, 2004, I left Fort Campbell, Kentucky, with an advanced party, and made the long trip over to Iraq. I kept wondering what was bothering me so much. I had been on numerous dangerous missions and had returned home safe and sound. I whispered a prayer.

Finally we arrived in Iraq on June 12. As we were unpacking, I noticed my friend Leo was taking a

book out of his bag. It was a philosophy book about the meaning of life. I silently prayed to God, asking Him to give me a chance to talk to Leo about Him.

Suddenly, broken glass and black billowing smoke were all around me. An enemy rocket had hit the side of the PX.

Since I was the Senior Noncommissioned Officer (NCO) on the ground at that time, Major Paul was showing me around the area. He had volunteered to go over with the advanced party to keep others from having to spend time away from their families. He would only be in Iraq for a couple more weeks. Then he would return home to his wife, their seven-year old son and six-week-old daughter.

After just a few days in Iraq, I ran out of shaving cream about halfway through my shave. I could not believe it! I would have to go over to the PX, the military general store, to purchase some, about a six-mile-round trip.

On the morning of June 16, I woke up and started looking for Major Paul. Maybe he would know someone who could drive me over to the PX. We were fortunate enough to have a satellite mess hall at our facility. None of us had ever been too excited about eating the food that had been brought over in thermoses. Any excuse was a good one to travel to a bona fide mess hall a few miles away. I joked with Major Paul about taking him out to lunch if he would give me a ride over to the PX to pick up some supplies. He was glad to do it. We talked Leo into going with us. We enjoyed a good lunch together at the mess hall. Major Paul shared with Leo and me about his family. He was excited about going home in a few days to spend a lot of quality time with his wife and children. Then about 1340, we headed over to the PX. I was in a little bit of a hurry since I had a meeting at 1400.

As the three of us walked across the gravel parking lot, we were about to step into the PX when I felt something in the back of my leg. It felt like someone had kicked me.

Suddenly, broken glass and black billowing smoke were all around me. An enemy rocket had hit the side of the PX. People were screaming and scrambling to safety. I was not able to walk. I kept grabbing my left leg to try to stop the pain.

As I fell into the PX, I touched my jaw and pulled my hand away. Blood was everywhere on me. It was streaming from my jaw and gushing out of my head. I somehow part squatted/part leaned on the floor.

As some of the customers came over to render aid, I heard Leo's voice; however, for some reason I could not turn my head to see him. I spotted his boot as he was telling me he was all right. He had taken on shrapnel, suffered a concussion and was seriously hurt, but he was able to walk. He began directing my treatment. He told me Major Paul was down in the parking lot, but they were working on him.

When the chaplain prayed with me, I thought about the scripture in Hebrews 12. I knew angels surrounded me.

As a combat lifesaver came over to survey the situation, he kept telling me to remain calm; that I would be okay. Even though my head was bleeding badly, I wanted him to look at my leg, because it felt like it might be a serious wound.

As he cut away the pants leg, he found two large holes in my leg. My buddy Leo began to direct him in what to do. He and some of the other guys grabbed things off the PX shelves and began to render first aid.

The medics arrived and put me on a stretcher to take me over to the E.R. triage. The field hospital was just across the street, so we were there fairly quickly. Thirty were wounded. Since some of them were more seriously wounded than I was, they put me over in a corner to wait.

Even though I was in a lot of pain, what worried me was that I had not seen Major Paul since the attack. A chaplain came over to see how I was doing. At my request, he prayed with me. I begged him to let me know how the Major was doing. Something told me Major Paul was gone. Later, when they were working on me, I was in quite a bit of pain and surrounded by sheer chaos. Doctors were yelling and people were scrambling to save as many lives as possible. In the midst of this pandemonium, the chaplain came over and told me the Major had not made it.

When the chaplain prayed with me, I thought about the scripture in Hebrews 12. I knew angels surrounded me. I did not feel the pain anymore. The doctors continued to work; yet they were not able to get the shrapnel out.

I looked down at my leg to see what they had been doing to it. I could not believe what I saw! As I focused on the rags that they had used as field expedient bandages, I saw words on them. My heart leaped. The words were from Psalm 91.

At that moment, I remembered Momma's words...

"Be good, be careful, and live for the Lord. I'm praying for you. I love you."   Momma

I remembered Psalm 91, verse 11.

"For He shall give His angels charge over you to keep you in all your ways."

I began to realize that God was speaking to me. I had always been in control, or so I thought, but God had really been in control all along. I had been in the most dangerous situations, yet I was never injured. How could this have happened when I was only going to get shaving cream at the PX? God was saying through this,

"You're not in control – I am. Let me take care of you."

When the medical personnel told me I was going to the hospital in Germany, I told them I wanted to take my Bible. While they were getting my belongings, I noticed that even though they had cut my clothes off and thrown away all the other bandages, the two Psalm 91 bandanas were still on the bed beside me. They had tied the two of them together to form the tourniquet, but instead of cutting them apart to remove them, they had untied them. I still have those two bloody bandanas today to attest to the fact that God saved my life.

The doctors in Germany seemed a little worried about the piece of shrapnel that was lodged in my jaw. The internal bleeding in my neck was extremely bad. It was swollen to the point that I could not move my neck. When they ran a CAT scan on my body, they discovered that the piece of shrapnel in my neck was dangerously close to the carotid artery, which supplies blood to the neck and head. I was assured that it would be a simple surgery, probably not more than 45 minutes. While I was out under the anesthesia, they would work on the other wounds.

During the surgery, I had a dream. I was surrounded by darkness. It was like I was floating, nothing
above me and nothing below me. I saw two gray lines
that appeared to meet in the distance. I heard God's
voice....

*"All things began with Me...and all things
ultimately lead to Me."*

At that moment, I saw my friend Leo in my dream.
He was saying, "Darrin, I want to know God."

When I awakened from the surgery, the doctors
were all looking at me with ashen faces. They told me it
was a miracle that I was alive. The piece of shrapnel in
my neck had pierced the sheathe of skin that surrounds
the carotid artery and was lodged between the artery
and the skin. It took them five hours to remove the piece
of shrapnel. Astonished, they said they could not have
placed it there with surgery. Just think—when the piece
of shrapnel flew into my neck from the explosion, there is
no telling what the speed of it was. The doctor was so
impressed, he gave me the piece of shrapnel to keep

I ended up sharing a hospital room with Leo. Leo
looked across the room from his hospital bed. He com-
mented, "You know, Darrin, I had the Bible shoved down
my throat all my life. I have lost close family members. I
have been a little angry with God, but all this didn't happen by accident. I think God wants to know me, and I want
to know God."

I began talking with Leo about God and told him about the dream. Then I began to share with him about Mere Christianity written by C.S. Lewis. I wanted to buy it for him when we returned to the States. Leo let me know he had seen them packing some books in my bag when we left Iraq. I asked the nurse to get my bag. The book was right on top, along with my Bible. As soon as we returned to Fort Campbell, Leo went to see the chaplain and gave his life to the Lord.

June 16, 2004, my life was radically changed in a few seconds. Life took on a different meaning. I am now looking forward to walking out the purpose God has for me.

Darrin spends much of his personal time speaking to churches, schools, and corporations – telling many of his amazing combat adventures and relational accounts while providing hope, encouragement and foundations for faith. For more information or for scheduling opportunities, please contact the Nashville Speakers Bureau at 866-333-8663, or www.nashspeakers.com.

Chapter 7

A Thousand May Fall

The Word of God in Psalm 91 as inscribed on the bandana was of tremendous comfort to me during my year's tour of duty in Iraq. As an International Peacekeeper serving in Baghdad, training and mentoring Iraqi Police, it was the most important piece of equipment that I carried on a daily basis—even more so than my M-4 assault rifle, my 9MM pistol, or my armored vest.

I always made sure I had my bandana with me before I headed out to work, traveling in a convoy, or deploying on a mission for the day. One particular day, as we were traveling to work through the Green Zone (also known as the International Zone), we went around some vehicles that were waiting in line at a crowded intersection. When we went around the line of cars, an explosion occurred in our rearview mirror. Well over 50 people were blown up and more than 100 injured. At the same time, an explosion was happening right beside us.

Many times the insurgents stage simultaneous attacks, trying to kill the rescuers and anyone else around. Many people were killed and injured that day all around us, but we weren't harmed in our vehicle. These people, mostly Iraqi guards, had just checked our identification at the gate. I believe that was the largest number of people ever killed around me.

The constant smell of gunpowder was continually in the air along with sights of destruction all around. When I was staying at a hotel in downtown Baghdad across the river from the Green Zone, a large demonstration outside our hotel took place with lots of shooting. People were coming over the walls with swords. I called my wife Ann and asked her to pray. I told her I was glad I had my bandana right there with me. I felt God's presence and protection as my wife and others were praying for me. I made it through without a scratch.

I just don't know how many times similar things have happened to me. In one instance, an IED, Improvised Explosive Device, was planted in a concrete planter on the 3rd ID Bridge. The IED exploded as we went by. Nobody was hurt or killed.

On a return trip to Mosul from Kurdistan, we came upon a twisted metal truck that had been carrying explosives meant for us, but the bomb prematurely detonated. Some small arms fire followed up. It was meant for us in the convoy, but they narrowly missed us.

I went to work every day on the most dangerous piece of highway in the world. Numerous times we came within seconds or minutes of being killed. In front of us or behind us, a bomb would go off or a sniper would

Photo provided by Donald Tate

Lt. Col. Steve Summey, Don Tate and Lt. Mahmood

shoot people. In all this, the words of Psalm 91 became life to me in the valleys of death that I traveled through.

Day and night brought the constant barrage of mortars, rockets, snipers, or suicide car bombers. Psalm 91 constantly allowed me to stay in contact with the Lord. Even though I saw others blown up and die to the right, left, front, and rear of me, I felt His hand of protection was upon me—an abiding under His wing. He is my Advocate and Defender. The Psalm 91 bandana wasn't just a piece of cloth. It was a symbol of the living Word of God with me and in me.

It was such a joy to see the Psalm 91 bandanas on the PX shelves available for others. It was unusual in that it was the only Christian item available in the PX. I was surprised and glad to see it. Many times everything has to be so politically correct that spiritual items are not allowed. I certainly did not want to be the only one in possession of the Word of God. With it on me, I had a knowing that I was neither forgotten nor alone as long as He was with me in all things and at all times of day and night—His angels on guard and at the ready.

The Psalm 91 bandana wasn't just a piece of cloth. It was a symbol of the living Word of God.

I felt the love of God was always with me. I was under His protection just as others were throughout the Bible—just as anyone can be who seeks Him. Without Him, it would have been impossible for me to stay focused and sane in a land and situation that did not make sense. In Iraq truly there are no atheists in foxholes, I can assure you. The reality check is overwhelming knowing that death and destruction are all around you—and wondering where it will strike next. The comfort and promises of God were the only true and consistent things that we had. Many times while we were under ambush and attack, I found comfort and peace in His Word.

In situations of life and death, knowing that you are not alone but under the wings of His divine protection cannot be described in any words spoken by a human being. The enemy (Satan) was constantly hunting around as a hungry lion seeking to devour and destroy. Some people talked about being in the wrong place at the wrong time; but the evidence is irrefutable of the miraculous things God has done.

It's important to understand that we do not have to depend upon fate for things to happen to us. God does not operate in a happenstance manner. He gives us promptings of what to do and where to go. He does not leave us in confusion. He is not a God of fear. The promises of God in the words of Psalm 91 are open to all who desire to believe and receive it in their hearts. I witnessed the bravery of all the young G.I.'s in Iraq, both young men and women, constantly in harm's way. For them not to be fully equipped would be such a disservice. Let the Word and works of God always be available to them in such things as the Psalm 91 bandana.

A thousand may fall at your side and ten thousand at your right hand but it shall not come near you.
Psalms 91:7

Donald Tate
U.S. State Department Advisor

Chapter 8

In Him I Will Trust

*T*his story was submitted by my dear friend, Gail
DeRouen. I have known Gail and Wesley for years
and think very highly of them. Wesley is a Vietnam veteran and wanted to do something to help our young soldiers. Through a series of circumstances, he was offered
a civilian job in Iraq. He accepted it and has been there
for almost a year. I saw him when he was on leave. He
proudly showed me his underlined Psalm 91 bandana.

    Wesley and I traveled to Houston where he was to
board a plane going to Iraq to begin his new job. As he
was packing, I added a Psalm 91 bandana that Jill had
given me to send with him. Wes asked me, "What's that
for?" I told him I wanted him to have this with him all the
time while he was overseas. I added that it had been
prayed over. I explained that God had given Jill the idea
of the bandanas to release protection to the military men
and women while in Iraq. Since he would be working
hand in hand with the military, I believed it was for him as
well. He said, "Okay. Put it in my suitcase."

When Wesley arrived in Iraq, he was positioned at Camp Cedar II, Iraq as a tanker truck driver. His first trip out on October 21 was driving for his CC (Convoy Commander). The CC's truck is the first one out of the gate and responsible for the convoy. Wesley was a little nervous, because he had not been in a war zone since he was in Vietnam. Wes had seen and been in an action environment while in Nam as a young man in his late teens to early twenties, but he was now a man of 55 on October 12, the day he flew out of the Houston airport—destination Iraq.

On October 21, the convoy left the gate traveling with 17 trucks. Suddenly they were ambushed. Wesley's heart raced as he saw and heard the blast. His CC was in radio contact with all the personnel as well as the military Humvees traveling with them. The report came in that 14 trucks had been ambushed. Four of them were no longer with the convoy. Wesley arrived at his destination unharmed to notice that only three trucks remained undamaged.

Wesley had stepped into a new place of faith because of a square piece of fabric.

When he returned to his base in Camp Cedar II, Wesley took his dirty clothes to the laundry room to be washed. He went about his duties. Then he remembered he did not have the Psalm 91 bandana on him. He went back to the laundry and asked if he could get his bandana. They told him he would have to look for it himself because of the tremendous amount of laundry dropped off daily. He started the search and found it. With a sigh of relief, he put it in his pocket. Wesley had stepped into a new place of faith because of a square piece of fabric—something to touch and to hold onto to remind him that God was with him.

At this point, Wes began to read Psalm 91 to the convoy each time they took a trip out. He believed God's Word would be protecting them. Because they were on a tight schedule, he underlined specific words to read over the convoy each time before they drove out of the gate. He knew God's Word was in his heart, but the covering of the Word on his person was like having the arms of God around him. Wesley will not get dressed without his Psalm 91 bandana on his person.

Thank God for this dream that God has given Jill. It has become an inspiration for many who may not be comfortable in church. They are wearing God's Word and trusting in His power to protect them. It reminds them that others are praying for them.

Chapter 9

Unsung Heroes

The military chaplains I have met or corresponded with over the past two years are some of the most honorable men and women I have ever had the pleasure to meet. They are totally committed to those in their charge and are constantly looking for ways to make things better for them. These are just a few of the chaplains with whom I have become acquainted.

Chaplain Robert Pleczkowski

Thank you, thank you, thank you!!! I really appreciate that you tracked me down and sent out the box of bandanas, cards and candy canes. The box arrived a couple of days before Christmas - so they were handed out as Christmas gifts to everyone here. You, and so many others, have been so kind and generous in your support to us here in Afghanistan. I am humbled and amazed!

I am attaching a photo of what I was able to pass out to each soldier through the chaplain's office through people's generosity. All things considered, it was a blessed Christmas here. Thank you again for keeping the soldiers and me in mind; I pray that God continues to use you and bless your work and ministry!

Robert Pleczkowski,

CH, MAJ Chaplain - JLC 180

(Father Bob)

Christmas Gifts for Soldiers in Afghanistan

Chaplain Dennis Goodwin

I am the Senior Chaplain or Brigade Chaplain for the first National Guard Combat Brigade to be mobilized to go to war since World War II. I purchased a Psalm 91 desert camouflage bandana at the Clothing Sales at

Fort Bragg, North Carolina and contacted the email address on the bandana to see how we might purchase more for our men and women who would soon be departing for Iraq. Jill Boyce was always encouraging and promised to help in any way she could to help us have as many bandanas as possible.

2003 Email from Chaplain Goodwin:

I am Chaplain (LTC) Dennis M. Goodwin, Brigade Chaplain for 4,500 mobilized National Guardsman from five states who will be deployed to Iraq early next year. Yesterday while at Military Clothing Sales on Ft. Bragg, NC, I was given one of your desert camouflaged handkerchiefs with Psalm 91 printed on it. How can I get more of these? I like it very much. It is something many of our soldiers would appreciate while in Iraq and would cherish. Any help you can offer would be much appreciated as we have no funds for procurement. Thank you for developing such a useful product!

Dennis M. Goodwin

I shared this hope with a member of Trinity United Methodist Church in Jacksonville, North Carolina where I served as the Senior Pastor prior to mobilization. Some of the businessmen in my church came together and purchased over 200 Psalm 91 bandanas to pass out to our men and women while in Iraq. I shared these bandanas on two occasions with the six chaplains who worked with me in Iraq, and all of us gave them out one at a time. Some chaplains gave special coins for support of their ministry. We did not have coins, but we sure did have Psalm 91 bandanas. So for acts of generosity supporting Christian ministry while in Iraq we gave each soldier a bandana.

We also reserved some bandanas for those men and women who performed a particularly kind deed for another soldier while deployed. The bandanas were always appreciated and revered. I brought about 50 back home with me and will now share them with two Navy chaplains with Marine Corps units from our church. I know they will be pleased. As the temperatures swell well over 100 degrees, these bandanas become a badge of encouragement and hope. God has certainly blessed this simple and practical article as Psalm 91 is well known as the Soldier's Psalm. May God continue to bless all who give and receive Psalm 91 in the form of a bandana.

Chaplain (LTC) Dennis M. Goodwin

Chaplain Brian Bohlman

While serving as a chaplain in the National Guard, I found the Psalm 91 bandana to be a great resource to make available to troops before leaving on a deployment. When service members understand the significance of

U. S. Army Photo by Spc. Brian Schroeder

*Many soldiers hung their Psalm 91 bandana on
the wall.*

Psalm 91 and the promise of God's protection, they all
want a bandana as a source of spiritual and physical
comfort while deployed. After my service in support of the
global war on terror, I had my bandana framed and
placed it in my office as a constant reminder to pray for
those serving in the U.S. Armed Forces.

When not serving in the military, I serve as the
president of the So Help Me God Project, a nonprofit organization that inspires faith, patriotism, and support of
our troops. The Psalm 91 bandana is one of our most

popular resources, with over 7,000 bandanas distributed since we teamed up with Jill Boyce in 2003. We recently conducted "Operation Thank You," a special military appreciation event at a local mall where shoppers stopped by to sign a thank you card and a Psalm 91 bandana to be sent to a deployed service member. It was a huge success!

I thank God for inspiring Jill to create the Psalm 91 bandana and for her faith to establish Wear the Word and Deployed Soldiers Family Foundation to see her dream come to life. I can only imagine the people Jill will meet in Heaven—who found God's peace and protection—when they placed their faith in the God who promises "long life" and "salvation" to all who "dwell in the secret place of the Most High." (Psalm 91:16)

For more information on the "So Help Me God" Project, or to order products call 866-645-6284 or go to www.SoHelpMeGod.org

Chaplain Martha Carson

I met Jill in February 2004 at my annual denominational conference for Chaplaincy Full Gospel Churches (CFGC) in Dallas. I was immediately impressed with the Psalm 91 bandanas she was introducing to the chaplains and others attending our meeting. I bought 100 (all she had left!) to take back to Fort Sill, Oklahoma, to give to deploying National Guard and Reserve soldiers. As a mobilized Reserve chaplain, my primary responsibility has been to serve as a chaplain for the National Guard and Reserve units who mobilized at Fort Sill to prepare for deployment to Iraq or other areas.

I gave out those 100 bananas the day after I returned to Fort Sill. The second half of a National Guard combat engineer battalion from Oklahoma was departing for Iraq that day. Since I had enough bandanas for less than half of those soldiers, I had 400 of them shipped to the chaplain in Iraq. Chaplain (then 1st LT) Pinkie Fischer is one of our CFGC chaplains. I also had bandanas shipped to Chaplain (MAJ) Lynn Wilson for a National Guard battalion from South Dakota since they had deployed weeks prior to my learning of the bandanas. I have given out over 2,000 bandanas since I met Jill.

One of the other mobilized Reserve chaplains, Chaplain (LT COL) Brenson Bishop, emailed me from Iraq, requesting I send him another bandana. He had given his to a young soldier who seemed anxious about going out on a convoy. Chaplain Bishop said after praying with the young man and giving him the bandana, he seemed much more at ease about the upcoming mission.

In October of 2004, I went to Geronimo's gravesite for a young Marine's reenlistment ceremony. The Apache Chief's grave in the Apache Cemetery is one of the most visited sites at Fort Sill. It was a picture-perfect day for such an outdoor gathering.

Visitors from other tribes sometimes leave certain items at the grave as an offering, including bandanas, which they hang in the cedar tree by the grave. Non-tribal visitors will also leave items by the grave or tied in the tree in their attempt to pay tribute to the Apache Chief.

I noticed one of the desert camouflage bandanas hanging in the tree! I went over to look at it and saw a soldier had written an inscription on it and dated it 17 August 2004. I smiled to myself when I realized he was one of the soldiers who had received a bandana from me just a few days prior to that date at his unit's farewell ceremony. That unit would have deployed for Iraq within days after he left his bandana as a tribute to the warrior from another era and culture.

On 8 November 2004, somewhere in Baghdad, that present-day warrior, a U.S. Army soldier, marched into eternity, as have countless warriors before him.

Chaplain Phil Glick

When I first developed the Psalm 91 bandana, I was under the impression that I should give the bandanas away. I never thought about selling them. Things changed when I realized I did not have the funds to purchase more, yet the demand for more was still there.

When I received an email request for bandanas

from Chaplain (MAJ) Phil Glick, I sat at my computer and cried. I did not understand why God would let this happen. I had done everything that I possibly knew to raise money, but the income for bandanas had simply dried up.

Looking back, I can see God's plan to provide sales in the Military Post Exchanges. For instance, Brigade Quartermasters never would have picked up the bandanas to wholesale to Post Exchanges if I had not been forced to sell them. Darrin Crowder would not have received the encouragement of God's Word on the military bananas used as field expedient bandages if they had not been for sale in his local PX in Iraq. At the time, it was difficult for me to see God's plan.

After the initial help of Chaplain Jim Combs who helped me get the first bandanas to service men and women at Fort Hood, I believe God opened the door to all the other stories in this book through Chaplain Glick, who eventually ordered over 300 bandanas for those in his care.

Dear Mrs. Boyce,

I was deeply moved by your last email and more committed than ever to find the funds back home. I've just arrived back from leave in Virginia and am happy to say that through a love offering taken in my church and others, that there are sufficient funds to order at least 330 bandanas.

I am very excited about being able to give this powerful reminder of God's presence to our soldiers and grateful to your wonderful ministry.

I look forward to hearing from you soon.

Chaplain Glick

Chaplain Glick recently told me that his soldiers wore the Psalm 91 bandanas around their necks, on top of their heads and in their back pockets. When he gave some out to Commanders in the Brigade Task Force, they received them with gratitude and treated the bandana as a special gift.

Chapter 10

Stories from Combat

Brian Shepherd's Story

I've kept my prayer cloth, the Psalm 91 bandana, under my helmet at all times, knowing that God's Word was over me and keeping me protected. I've been nearly blown up by roadside bombs about four or five times. At other times, the roadside bombs didn't go off, and many times we've driven past roadside bombs that were some-how forgotten. There's no telling how many very danger-ous situations we were in and didn't even know about.

Our company was protected and blessed through 365 days going into the most dangerous areas in Bagh-dad, during some of the most dangerous times. We were out and about in Baghdad every day of the year, and we only lost two people. We've been in numerous fire-fights, had rocket propelled grenades launched at us, real rockets launched at us, and encountered numerous car bombs. As a company, we've been blown up by roadside bombs over 50 times, and we still came back minus two people that were tragically taken away.

By God's grace, we were named the best military police unit in Iraq. The battles that we were in are documented in the military police history books. In fact, the tactics that we used in the battles are being taught to new military policemen. The Psalm 91 bandana that you sent to us was like feeling the Word Himself over us. That is the consensus of the people who I've hung around and talked to.

Sergeant Chuck Hreha's Story

Remember Sergeant Chuck Hreha, the one whose wife Karen asked for bandanas for his unit before deploying in early January, 2004? I recall how touching it was to hand these to the guys, knowing that they were going over to Iraq in just a few days.

Photo provided by Karen Hreha

Chuck Hreha, center, in formation at Color Casing Ceremony

I talked to Chuck after he returned from about 14 months of deployment. He told me that when he was on gate guard duty, he kept his Psalm 91 bandana in his Kevlar, bulletproof combat helmet. The Kevlars currently are used by the ground troops. He said he arranged it inside his helmet with most of the words showing so that he could pull his Kevlar off to read the words anytime he wanted. He told me that at the time, several IEDs, Improvised Explosive Devices, were going off and suicide bombers were blowing up gates.

"Thank you for giving me something that wasn't bulky that I could keep with me to always keep God on my mind."
Sergeant Charles Hreha

Chuck added that his wife Karen, a teacher in a local Christian School, had one of the bandanas up in her classroom while Chuck was gone. It reminded her and her students to pray for him and the others who were in harm's way. Many of Karen's students and the other students in the school had parents overseas.

Staff Sergeant Monte Hayden

After giving his testimony, Chuck handed the phone to Staff Sergeant Monte Hayden who wanted to say a little something. He talked about how important it was to have items like dog tags and bandanas from home that reminded him that people were praying for him. He said he also folded under the corners of the bandana and placed it in his helmet so he could read the Psalm 91 words from time to time.

"Whether I wore it on my head or had it in my hand, I felt safer. It reinforced my belief in Christ and helped me stay on track."

Staff Sergeant Monte Hayden

Lieutenant Colonel Noriega's Story

I'm still getting wonderful notes, packages and emails. Probably one of the most interesting things that happened over the past couple of months is how much a particular scripture played in my life. Way back when I was first deployed, Carolyn Shaver, a family friend of my wife Melissa, shared with me about Psalm 91, sometimes known as "A Soldier's Prayer." I didn't think much about it again until my swearing in. I brought my Bible that my in-laws, the Meisgeiers, had given me. It was important to me to take my oath with this Bible. I had turned the pages to a scripture that Melissa had given me when we first started dating, Isaiah 58. I placed my hand on Isaiah 58 to take my oath.

Major Eyre, who was holding my Bible, had turned to another scripture, Psalm 91. I asked him what he was doing and he merely replied, "Trust me," and I did. Later, I went back and studied the Psalm. During that week, I was sharing with my father-in-law that I had taken my oath on the Bible given to me by them. I told him that Major Eyre had flipped the pages to Psalm 91, "A Soldier's Prayer." He said, "Oh, that's the Psalm your dad prays and reads for you every day."

I was stunned and touched. This week, I received a letter and a desert camouflage bandana from Carolyn with the "Soldiers Prayer," Psalm 91, printed on it. I carry the printed bandana now every day in my back pocket. Some days you gotta' know you're blessed.

I found this story on the Internet (evidently written soon after Rick Noriega arrived in Afghanistan). I recognized my friend Carolyn's name, contacted her, and emailed Rick. He adds this note:

Just as a follow-up, my in-laws, Connie and Charles Meisgeier, took up a collection from friends and sent me 100 bandanas. I have distributed them to the soldiers in my unit. With the hot dusty months upon us, soldiers wear them as scarves to protect their faces. Many of them have the scarves hung on their walls.

Then again, some soldiers like myself just fold the Psalm 91 bandana and carry it every day in their back pocket. Thanks for the blessed intervention that has touched so many.

Lieutenant Colonel Richard Noriega
Afghanistan

Miles' Story
(As told by his mother)

Dear Jill,
I wanted to thank you for providing such a comforting reminder of God's presence to our young airmen in the Middle East. This is our son Miles wearing your bandana. He is stationed in the Air Force in the Middle East. Unfortu-

Miles wearing his bandana

nately, I cannot say exactly where he is. Miles is 21 years old and volunteered for this assignment because he felt it was a worthwhile cause, and God would be with him. He played guitar in the praise band at our little church in Fredericksburg, Virginia. A lovely lady whose husband Mike had been in Vietnam gave your bandana to Miles just before he left on this assignment. She said it would comfort him as he faced dangerous times. Her sweetness and your precious creation brought tears to my eyes and those of many mothers in our church.

Miles wears his bandana every day and tells me, "Mom, I know the Lord sees me down here and smiles, because He loves to see His holy words as He looks down from Heaven."

I have just ordered another bandana for a young man who is just out of high school and going into the Marines. I pray he feels the same comforting peace as my son Miles.

Thank you for doing this wonderful work, I will remember you all in my prayers.

May the Lord bless the work of your hands and keep you always.

Judy Murray

Onna's Story

Dear Jill,

Last year after my nephew was deployed to Iraq, I purchased several of your bandanas to send to him and to give to our family members. As I was taking his younger brother to the airport in Little Rock, I saw a soldier approaching. My nephew and I moved down so that he could have a place to sit. He said he was going for his second tour back to Iraq. We chatted for a while, and he told us that he had been wounded severely the first time, shot in the head. We gave him a bandana and told him how thankful we were for him and all the men and women who are fighting for us. He got really emotional at that

Tanks on Convoy

U.S. Army Photo by Brian Schroeder

Not Afraid

point and told me that he had had one of those Psalm 91
bandanas in his helmet when he got shot! And the good
Lord let him live to tell the tale! I told him this one would
keep him safe too! His outfit was in one of the most dangerous situations over there, and he had lost a lot of men.
His name is Sergeant Woods. I am still praying for his
safety. Our nephew made it home in March 2005, safe
and sound. God bless you all.

Onna Newell

Saved from the Fire
(Submitted by Pat Flynn)

My brother was deployed to Iraq in February of 2004. He
is in the Air National Guard, but he and a group of four
others were chosen to train and work for the Army, driving
missions all over Baghdad and the general area. They
were gunners on the convoys. It was a very difficult time
for me. I worried constantly for his safety. I prayed for him
and everyone else in Iraq each day, but it just did not
seem to be enough.

Then I received my July 2004 Guideposts magazine with an article about the Psalm 91 bandanas. This
article had a big impact on me. I really felt this was something I had to do for my brother and the people who
served with him. I ordered 25 of the bandanas. My husband and I wrote a message of encouragement on each

tag. We included our email address in case anyone desired to contact us. I remember that it was just before the Fourth of July.

For my brother, I wrote a special message and included the story from <u>Guideposts</u> so he would know how the bandanas came to be. I was very excited to mail the box. I had the feeling that somehow these would help to comfort him and whoever he gave them to. I felt it would help them truly feel God's presence, 24/7. I made a copy of one of the bandanas and placed it in a patriotic display that I had in my foyer. The prayer warmed my heart every time I read it, and I felt a little less afraid for my brother.

He got really emotional at that point and told me that he had had one of those Psalm 91 bandanas in his helmet when he got shot.

He appreciated receiving the bandanas and gave them out to the men and women in his group. I sensed I had truly done something that would help these soldiers cope better while they were in Iraq. I discovered a few months later there was even more to the story than I had ever dreamed.

My husband and I received the following email in February, 2005 from Air Force Staff Sergeant Adam Megginson, known among his peers as "Preacher" or

"Rev.," because he was usually the one who led prayer. He told us later that even though they were in very dangerous situations, God brought them through and kept them strong. In fact, their platoon didn't have a single loss or injury.

From: Adam Megginson
Sent:Wednesday, Feb. 16, 2005
Subject: Psalm Bandanas

Mr. and Mrs. Flynn,

I wanted to write and thank you for the Psalm 91 bandanas you purchased and sent to Iraq. You are probably thinking that was a long time ago, but your gift went a long way. I don't know exactly when these were sent. I was given a stack of these bandanas from a guy that was leaving for home, when I had just arrived. I went back to my group and passed them out to all who wanted them. I was surprised at some of the folks who wanted a bandana. With the line of work that we were doing, driving the roads of Iraq, we wanted our hands on every bit of encouragement that we could get.

Your gift certainly helped us. People who came in later asked where we got them. Eventually we were able to buy them on base. Mine hung with my American flag on the wall. Some people just used them as a bandana, but God's Word was always there.

In one incident, it stood strong. We had a truck that was hit by a large car bomb. Luckily, the truck was armored and everyone walked away, but the truck was not so lucky. As the car burned, the truck caught fire. It burned hot enough to melt and burn everything inside the truck. The fire even caused ammo to explode in the boxes and melt bulletproof glass. When the truck was recovered, the only things found inside that weren't steel were half of a Kevlar helmet, a small piece of a uniform and a Psalm 91 bandanna. All the edges were burned, but the message remained intact. It is a powerful message to show Who is really in charge in any situation. The last I heard there was talk of it going home to be framed. We are home now, and the rest will be home soon. If I go again, you can be sure that the bandana will be first among the things I pack. So thanks again for your support. It meant more than you'll ever know.

Staff Sergeant Adam Megginson

Chapter 11

Thoughts from Loved Ones

God's Protection – Carrie Crowder

When my son Darrin was first deployed overseas, I worried about him but tried not to show it. I wrote to him about the hometown news and what was going on at church or with the family. In each letter, I always gave him a scripture. Many times it was the 91st Psalm. I felt like Psalm 91 was my assurance that God was protecting my son.

The room Darrin grew up in became a prayer room, because when I felt concerned, I would take my Bible and kneel by Darrin's bed. I asked God to help me pray. He would always lead me to a scripture. After I prayed, I would write out the scripture and put it on the refrigerator with a magnet. I remember when I wrote out Psalm 91 and attached it. I knew God had given His angels charge over Darrin.

Darrin had been in dangerous places all over the world. When he was in Afghanistan, we didn't hear from him for several weeks, but I had an assurance that he was all right. This time was different. I could not shake the feeling that something was not right. I had always prayed for Darrin when he was overseas. This time, I prayed constantly.

When Darrin came home, he showed me the two bloody bandanas the medics had used as tourniquets and the piece of shrapnel that the doctors had removed...I knew that it was no coincidence.

One night soon after he had gone over to Iraq, I had a feeling that something was going to happen. I could not sleep. I prayed through the night. The next day, Darrin called his sister Denyne to tell her he had been wounded. He asked her to let me know. Later that day, I received official word from Fort Campbell about Darrin's condition. They were flying him to a hospital in Germany for further treatment.

Darrin called me from Germany the following day. He sounded weak, but I was glad to hear his voice. He told me that the emergency team had used two Psalm 91 military bandanas tied together as a tourniquet for his leg. The doctor told Darrin his life was miraculously saved. I just praised the Lord because this was my Psalm—one that I had prayed over Darrin many times and sent to him in letters. I would always write the same thing at the end of my letters...

"Be good, be careful, and live for the Lord.
I'm praying for you. I love you.
~ Momma."

When Darrin came home, he showed me the two bloody bandanas the medics had used as tourniquets and the piece of shrapnel that the doctors had removed— the piece of shrapnel that would have instantly ended his life if God hadn't intervened. I knew that it was no coincidence that they had used Psalm 91 to bind his wounds. God wanted to show us all that He is still God and that He is still in control.

Closer to God - Mary Martinez

Mary Martinez, wife of Staff Sergeant Michael Martinez, serves as Vice President of Deployed Soldiers Family Foundation and has been acting as Fort Hood liaison since March of 2004. Her friend told her about the Psalm 91 bandana, and we became acquainted.

Before my husband Michael deployed, a friend of mine informed me, "I've got something to give you, but I cannot give it to you until my husband returns from serving in Iraq." When her husband returned, she presented me with a Psalm 91 bandana that she had kept next to her husband's picture.

I decided to carry on the tradition. When Michael deployed, I placed that same Psalm 91 bandana next to his picture in our living room. It gave me comfort to know He was in God's hands. I am proud of my husband and glad he could serve our country, but I still felt helpless and worried. Having the bandana helped.

After Michael deployed, I decided to purchase a bandana for him to have with him in Iraq. I emailed Jill to find out how to order. Then in March, 2004, we finally talked on the phone. That's when I ordered two bandanas for my husband. I sent him an extra one so that he could always have one with him while the other one was being washed.

This had such an impact on my husband that he returned home a different man. He has never been a fan of organized religion. When he came home from Iraq, he bought a study Bible and reads it all the time. He looks up Bible verses on the Internet. I really think having the Psalm 91 bandana with him helped him somehow find a closer relationship with God when he was overseas.

A Father's Perspective
Chief Warrant Officer (CW5) R. Keith Lane
US Army Reserve Command

I came from a military home with my dad serving as a Marine in WWII. I served in Vietnam as a young man. With this background, fear and pride crept through me as our oldest son told us he would be deploying to Iraq in a couple of months. In these times, when our country struggles with the issues of terrorist threats at home and war abroad, men and women continue to go so they can to do their part in keeping our homeland safe. From that aspect, I am very proud that my son will have a part in that effort.

Our son is a helicopter pilot in Iraq as I was in Vietnam. I know the dangers of flying low and slow over enemy territory. However, I had the luxury of having a jungle below to shield me from view until the last second. In the desert, there is no visibility restriction, and it worries me a great deal to know my son will be a target for every rebel with a gun or rocket launcher. The one thing that keeps me well grounded is my faith in God that my son will come back safe when his tour is done.

I wear the bandana every day. I have it stuffed in the top of my helmet so it has to go everywhere I do—even when I fly.

Brian Lane

Keith and Brian Lane
Father and Son

I have learned over the years that God is a great God. He answers prayers and cares for me like no other. When I was in war, God looked out for me. Though my helicopter was often hit by 20 or more bullets, I was never shot down. Only one crewmember was ever hit but not seriously injured.

Now our son is in God's hands.... He couldn't be any better off if I was there with him to watch out for him.

Oh, God, our great Creator, we lift up our voices to You in praise and thanksgiving for the love You have for us. Though we are unworthy at times, You forgive us. We are weak, but You Strengthen us; afraid but You comfort us.

Lord, we come to You now in our need and ask Your blessing upon our boys and girls who strive to serve our country and protect us from those who would do us harm. Protect them, Lord, and give them Your strength to endure and Your love to give them peace of mind.

For those of us left behind at home, give us also peace and comfort. Let us know of Your love for us and our children, with the reassurance we need to get through until they return to our embrace, and give our hearts rest.

These things we ask in Your Son's name, even Jesus.
Amen

Home Safe – Cathy Brooks

This was the most difficult time my husband and I have ever experienced. The "not knowing" was the hardest. We spent many nights walking the floors or driving the roads, just waiting to hear something, anything that would reassure us that our son was okay.

It was easier to watch the news and know what was going on than "not knowing." We are very proud of our son, but this is not something that we want to live through again any time soon. We give God the praise for returning our son home safely.

Our son is the fourth generation of Brooks to serve this great nation of ours during wartime. He has a strong support system through family, friends, and church, but other soldiers may not have this support. It is our duty as American citizens to provide support to as many soldiers as possible. They are putting their lives in danger to ensure that we continue to have freedom in the U.S.A., and we must show our support to the soldiers and their families in as many ways as possible.

Chapter 12

Angels Among Us

Cathy Brooks – Georgia SOAR Chapter

Cathy Brooks is the President of the Georgia Chapter of SOAR (Support Our American Recruits), a nonprofit organization that supports America's military here at home and overseas. SOAR works with schools and organizations to help teach children patriotism. Cathy teaches at Chatsworth Elementary in Chatsworth, Georgia and oversees the sending of care packages to all branches of the military. The children help collect and package not only personal care items and Christmas cards for the soldiers, but they also include Psalm 91 bandanas. Cathy says she could not do this work without her husband Billy, a Vietnam veteran, who helps her package up boxes and get them to the post office in his spare time.

My daughter-in-law met Jill at Fort Hood when she was selling bandanas in the mall of the PX in the fall of

2003. She purchased a couple of bandanas from Jill –
one for my son, a captain in the 1st Cavalry, and one for
me. She told Jill about how I send packages to the soldiers on a regular basis to encourage them. As soon as I
received my Psalm 91 bandana, I contacted Jill to purchase some to send to the troops.

Since that time, we have sent out well over 5,000
bandanas. A special lady in our town (who is now de-
ceased) purchased 2,000 to be sent to Iraq. She worried
about the soldiers who would not get a bandana and
wanted to make sure that as many soldiers as possible
would get one.

I teach reading in a very patriotic school, Chatsworth Elementary, and we strive to support our country
and service people in as many ways as possible. Our
school takes time on special holidays to show our love
and support for our great nation and our military troops.

It's not just our school that's been helping with this
effort. We've had the support of the entire community.
People from all across Murray County and Whitfield
County have been very supportive.

Please join with us and show your support to the
soldiers by giving to local groups that are sending care
packages to the troops. Some family members do not
have the funds to send necessary items to their loved
ones. It is our responsibility to help provide for their
needs. The cards and letters mean a lot to them, too. One
chaplain wrote…

I wanted to thank all of you for all the wonderful cards, emails, packages and prayers that you have sent my way over the past months. As always, morale dramatically increases with the arrival of mail.

It does not matter how much, or how little you can do for our troops. Anything and everything is appreciated when you are far away from home and loved ones. Our soldiers need to know that we love and support what they are doing and are waiting to welcome them home.

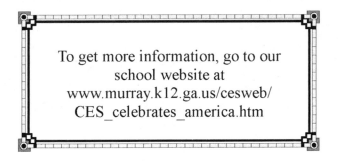

To get more information, go to our school website at
www.murray.k12.ga.us/cesweb/
CES_celebrates_america.htm

Nicky Blakeney

One of my favorite "angels" is a lady from Mississippi named Nicky Blakeney. She read about the Psalm 91 bandana in Guideposts magazine in the July, 2004 issue. She called me to order bandanas for some Mississippi

National Guard members who would soon be leaving to go overseas. During a luncheon held in honor of some of those leaving from Taylorsville and McGee, Mississippi, Nicky talked about the bandanas. That day, she received her first donation for bandanas—$100.

Nicky soon called me with an order for bananas to give out to troops who were shipping off for training at Camp Shelby, Mississippi. The order had been delayed. It had to be shipped overnight to get to Nicky in time for delivery to the troops before leaving for training. First, she would drive 50 miles to Richland to pick up the package of hundreds of bandanas. Then she would drive to two different locations several miles apart where the soldiers were departing. When she reached the town of McGee with the bandanas, she and her family members made their way through the crowd to give them out to her son-in-law's unit. The commander called Nicky's son-in-law up front to have him hand out the bandanas as the men were in formation.

Nicky watched as young men kneeled down on the floor and started folding their bandanas so they could wear them immediately. A sergeant said, "I don't know about you guys, but I need this." The servicemen hugged her in gratitude.

At the Taylorsville National Guard Armory, Nicky almost missed a chance to give out the bandanas. The men were already on the truck, but they gladly received the gifts from Nicky and her family. One young man who was seeing off both his older brother and his own twin brother helped hand out the bandanas. When asked, "Who are you?" Nicky answered, "These are from the people of Smith County." Many hugged her neck.

Nicky has sent bandanas to people as far away as South Carolina and Kentucky. She says she is still giving them out to soldiers as they leave for training or to go overseas. She gave one to a young lady for her fiancée who is serving in Iraq. When he received it, friends asked him where he got it. He sent word home that he would like to have some Psalm 91 bandanas for his friends. Nicky gave the young lady a dozen. Immediately she sent them over to the soldiers. She has now given out over 700 bandanas.

> *"I think I've received more blessings from giving out the Psalm 91 bandanas than anyone else."*

"I think I've received more blessings from giving out the Psalm 91 bandanas than anyone else. This is what I do. It's just a way of life for me. If I see a soldier in desert camos, I ask if he's coming home or going. Then I give him a bandana. I still carry one in my purse and several in my car in case I see a service man or woman who wants one. Since we live close to Camp Shelby, we often see soldiers in the mall and around town. We always thank them for what they are doing for our country."

Nicky Blakeney

Carmen Hawes – Hearts Away From Home

I came to know Carmen through a customer and friend, Elvena Badeker, who attends the same church as Carmen. Elvena ordered several Psalm 91 bandanas to add to the packages that Carmen and Hearts Away From Home were sending out to soldiers. Hearts Away From Home is a local ministry for members of Sylvan Oaks Christian Church in Citrus Heights, California, who have friends or relatives serving overseas in the military.

Hearts Away From Home had sent several bandanas to each of the soldiers on their list so that they could give them to others in their group. Carmen shared with me that when her nephew Shannon was over in Iraq, he went out on several dangerous missions. In spite of this, he was not worried, because he knew the Lord was taking care of him. He took the bandanas sent to him by his aunt and gave them out to others.

The excerpts below are from the Hearts Away From Home newsletter from October of 2004. Carmen shares, "The following letter is the Hearts Away From Home mission statement in action. Shannon Campbell, the author of the letter, is an Army Specialist serving in Iraq. I was blessed with the opportunity to help Shannon with shipments of water and supplies after his mess hall was blown up last spring by terrorists. The experience was the inspiration for this ministry. Our grassroots effort is now giving birth to our mission of sending Christ's love to our soldiers in the Middle East."

Dear Carmen,

Thank you for the packages you and your family have sent. Everything you sent is wonderful. I can't even begin to explain the boost of morale a soldier receives when he or she hears their name at mail call. Thank you once again. My brothers in arms will keep you, your family and your church in our prayers as well. God bless, and keep fighting the good fight (of faith) for the Lord.

Thank you,
Shannon Campbell

Thank you, Shannon, for not only serving on the battle-field, but also for serving on a mission field while on military tour in Iraq. We have heard of your faith in the Lord even through the difficult circumstances of war, and about sharing your faith with other soldiers. May the Lord bless you and bring you safely home to your family soon.

Carmen Hawes

Carmen says it's important to do what we can with what is in our hands. I agree. Any church, large or small, can do something for the troops. What I like about their method is they encourage the soldiers in their care to do the same by sending them multiples of each item—like the bandanas. Carmen says the goal of Sylvan Oaks

Christian Church is to keep sending out packages as long as men and women are being deployed overseas.

Celeste Mann – Army Mom

Celeste Mann is the choir director at St. Mary's Catholic Church in McHenry, Illinois. I recently met her through her friend, Darlene Mrachek, who had previously bought bandanas. I consider Celeste an "angel" because of her deep commitment to the military troops and her constant prayer for them.

After Celeste saw one of the Psalm 91 bandanas, she called to order several for her daughter Christine's unit in Iraq. Celeste shared with me that God had miraculously saved Christine's life on her first tour of duty in Iraq. Now she would be serving her second tour. Darlene Mrachek, the church organist, had sent her a Psalm 91 bandana in the mail. Christine cried when she opened the package and held the bandana in her hand.

She immediately contacted her mom, "I need to get these for my friends." Celeste decided to find a way to order for all 120 of the people in Christine's transportation unit. Celeste called me with her idea of raising money at her church through a choir concert. I agreed it was a great idea and told her I would be praying for her.

Just a short time later, Celeste called me to announce that the St. Mary's Adult Choir had raised enough money through their concert for every person in

Christine's unit to have a bandana! Celeste was able to order more than enough bandanas and found a unique way to get them to her daughter.

Christine decided to spend her two weeks of leave in Germany. Her mom met her there and took the bandanas with her. The response from one of Christine's friends was, "Thank you, Ma'am. I'll be proud to wear it."

Christine cried when she opened the package and held the bandana in her hand.

Celeste remarked that she had been praying and that God will continue to watch out for them. Because of the daily mortar fire, fear was all around them. They had all lost friends in the war. Celeste's words were valuable.

Back at home, Celeste found out about a soldier in her hometown who was called to go back for a second tour in Iraq. His wife and children were having a hard time dealing with the news. She presented a Psalm 91 bandana to the soldier and another one to his family to keep while he was away. They were moved by her gift and were encouraged. "Now we know Daddy will be safe because he has one, too."

The Gifts – Linda Martin

About two years ago, I met Jill Boyce at a Bible study at Ginnie Johnson's home in Dallas, Texas. Last Thanksgiving, I was preparing to visit my son Larry who worked at Ramstein Air Force Base, south of Frankfurt in Germany. As I relate the events that unfolded surrounding my departure, I believe you will see the hand of God at work. We plan things, but God, in His infinite wisdom, carries us beyond our own plans.

God put it on my heart to go and pray for the wounded soldiers at Landstuhl Hospital in Germany while I was visiting my son there.   A few months before I left for Germany, as I began to tell other people about my upcoming trip, people wanted to pray for me, and many wanted to contribute funds for telephone calling cards and other items I planned to take with me to give to the soldiers. Jill volunteered to provide me with about 50 Psalm 91 bandanas to give the soldiers also. I had my grandson Bryce Bogie, age 7, sign some of the bandanas because God has given him a special place in his heart to pray for the protection of the soldiers. I had others sign the bandanas and write messages and scripture on them.

I asked my son if he thought I could get on base to visit the hospital. He told me that because of the terrorist activities and so many things going on that I probably wouldn't be able to go there without the permission of the base commanders. He would check with them and see if anything could be done.

In the meantime, my Bible study friends and I prayed diligently that God would open doors for me to minister. We know with Him all things are possible, and if He is sending us on a divine mission, nothing is going to stop us. I knew God had prepared the way as I journeyed to Germany.   My son had gained permission for me to visit the hospital. Maggie, a friend of his, escorted me in. I had made up packets containing all the donated items including the Psalm 91 bandana for each of the soldiers I would visit.

As I went to different floors, I asked the soldiers if I could pray for them. I saw about twenty of them that night. They never said no to prayer, and when I asked what they would like me to pray for other than their physical healing, they ALL said their fellow soldiers who were still there in Iraq. I had prayed each soldier would get the right packet since all the bags contained Psalm 91 bandanas signed by different people back home in the United States. One young man from Indiana got the first packet I gave, which contained the bandana my grandson signed. I explained how special this was.

I could see that there were more than just physical injuries but a lot of emotional turmoil in the eyes of the wounded. Some soldiers knew they were going home. Others knew they had to go back to Iraq. But, they were of one heart and mind—still with their buddies on the front line.

I could not distribute all the packets that evening, but I went to the Air Force base and the Army base and handed out packets with the bandanas and notes. I thanked the soldiers and told them how much I appreciated them. I received the greatest gift—a blessing from God in being able to minister to soldiers who have given of themselves for our country.

Joe Swift – Tennessee Veterans

When I read the story of the Psalm 91 bandana in Guideposts magazine last summer, I began thinking about how to get bandanas to our Tennessee National Guard, the 278th Armored Cavalry, who were preparing to deploy to Iraq. I am in a couples' Sunday school class made up of 80% veterans of the Korean conflict and World War II. I mentioned to the class that furnishing bandanas for local members of the 278th Armored Cavalry would make a good class project. These men and women are from all over the state of Tennessee.

I called Jill and ordered 300 bandanas to get the project started. My pastor Doug Sager is a patriot, and he put a committee together to help. The next Sunday at church our Sunday school class members stood at the church doors with steel helmets used as collection plates for donations to the cause. We raised more than enough that day to purchase bandanas for all 4,000 members of the Tennessee National Guard. It amazed us to start with such a little idea and see it blossom.

Our class was then presented with a logistics problem. The Guard members needed the bandanas for a special ceremony. They wanted to give them out to the men and women while in formation before shipment overseas. We knew we had to get them there quickly. Jill's supplier, Brigade Quartermasters, just about turned back flips to get the bandanas to us on time. When they arrived, our Sunday school class worked until almost 11:00 at night packing the bandanas, the accompanying poem cards and a letter of thanks from the church into envelopes for the troops. The packages arrived just in time for the commander to give out the bandanas at the ceremony.

To our fellow Tennesseans, the 278th Armored Cavalry Regiment,

We here at home are proud of your service to our country. The Fletcher Holley, Beverly Swift, Bill Castilaw Sunday school class will be with you in spirit and in prayer throughout your service time. Our Sunday school class is composed of more than 80% veterans or participants in the World War II and Korean conflicts. We really do understand the sacrifices. Many of the veterans in our group carried a New Testament with a thin steel front plate during our service time. As you well know, this thin steel plate provided very little protection. However the New Testament was of great comfort to us in having God's Word close to our hearts.

Our church, First Baptist of Concord, is sending you a military bandana with The Soldiers Prayer, Psalm 91, printed on it. This scripture has been comforting soldiers of all generations. We hope it will be of comfort to you.

We wish to be available to you after you are deployed in the country. For any needs or prayer requests you may have, please contact our 278th coordinator.

Sent with our prayers and gratitude from the membership of First Baptist of Concord, Knoxville, Tennessee

After the men and women deployed, we received many emails and requests for bandanas from family members of those deployed. Since then, we've ordered and given away over 300 bandanas to family members. In responses from the soldiers, they have asked for prayer more than anything else.

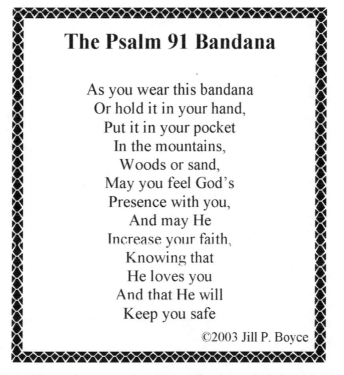

The Psalm 91 Bandana

As you wear this bandana
Or hold it in your hand,
Put it in your pocket
In the mountains,
Woods or sand,
May you feel God's
Presence with you,
And may He
Increase your faith,
Knowing that
He loves you
And that He will
Keep you safe

©2003 Jill P. Boyce

The Psalm 91 Bandana Poem Card is included with each bandana Jill sends out.

A Word from Jill...

Since the day I dreamed I was in Iraq, a fire has burned within me to help our deployed soldiers in any way that I can. Distributing the Psalm 91 bandanas is my way of lighting a candle in the darkness rather than cursing it. I pray that every person who reads this book finds a way to help. This may not be your particular mission from the Lord, but you can do something.

Children write letters and make cards. Churches send packages. Families pray, support and welcome their loved ones home. Companies and organizations support with programs, funds and volunteers. Airport travelers say "thank you" to soldiers passing through, and some even give them their first class seats on flights. Citizens applaud these uniformed men and women in restaurants, hotels and other public places. They send them phone cards, snacks, dog tags, books, bandanas, and Bibles. Many proudly display their American flags, place support-the-troops magnets on their vehicles, and cry when they say the Pledge of Allegiance or sing the National Anthem.

Since September 11, 2001, our country has been forever changed. War was inevitable. It came to us. It mocked us on our doorsteps and taunted us in our peaceful homes. Now, we have answered it with brave men and women who signed up, knowing their lives were now fragile.

Some have returned home safe and sound, with only nightmares to haunt them. Others were severely wounded and must deal with the consequences. Then there are the ones who came back in flag-draped caskets, their families forever torn. War is not pretty. It's not sweet. But the alternative may be our land blackened with fire and smoke much like that of the Twin Towers and the Pentagon of 9/11/01. You may not agree with this view of our times, but at least you can recognize the darkness and light a candle. Please join me in supporting our troops and their families.